VIGLETS
Ode to Dumbness

Viggo P. Hansen

authorHOUSE®

AuthorHouse™
1663 Liberty Drive
Bloomington, IN 47403
www.authorhouse.com
Phone: 1-800-839-8640

© *2011 Viggo P. Hansen. All rights reserved.*

No part of this book may be reproduced, stored in a retrieval system, or transmitted by any means without the written permission of the author.

Published by AuthorHouse 12/15/2011

ISBN: 978-1-4670-6245-9 (sc)
ISBN: 978-1-4670-6246-6 (e)

Library of Congress Control Number: 2011919462

Printed in the United States of America

Any people depicted in stock imagery provided by Thinkstock are models, and such images are being used for illustrative purposes only. Certain stock imagery © Thinkstock.

This book is printed on acid-free paper.

Because of the dynamic nature of the Internet, any web addresses or links contained in this book may have changed since publication and may no longer be valid. The views expressed in this work are solely those of the author and do not necessarily reflect the views of the publisher, and the publisher hereby disclaims any responsibility for them.

Dedication

Harkin fellow pilgrims
Evolution has taken a new tack
We are no longer a planet of apes
But a planet of dummies
Ha-La-Lu-Ja.

Viglets Two is dedicated to Dumbness in general and Dummies in particular, along with all the rest who have made being dumb an attractive and successful life style. It is now a scientifically acknowledged fact - dummies have indeed inherited the earth.

In earlier historical times this was not fully recognized, there was a glimmer of hope that it wasn't going to be true. Sadly we now know better. Dumbness reigns along with global warming.

The Society for the Advancement of Dummies (SAD) recently announced breaking news that:

Dummies are no longer
On our list of endangered species
Which is great news for all political
Office seekers.

However, curb your enthusiasm and keep in mind:

*Though dummies are no longer endangered
They are protected by laws of the land
That mercifully prevents their extermination
So the best we can all do
Is to join and celebrate each other
Because we are all here to stay – as dummies.*

Today we thrill and memorialize dummies' resurgences' and celebrate their creative handiwork, especially in business, education, religion and politics; now referred to as - Dummy BERP.

*Dummies are the happiest people on earth.
They never look back with regret
Their future beckons them with more dumbness
As they gleefully anticipate getting dumber
Life just keeps getting better and better
This of course means dumber and dumber.*

Furthermore, and with more appropriate compassion -

*Dummies are wonderful people
Neither subtle
Nor complex
What you see
Is what you get!*

It is with respectful enthusiasm for dummies and dumbness that this Viglet Two book is dedicated. Dummies – all of us - are inspirational and the future.

Viggo P. Hansen

One Dummy

Introduction

While Viglets One provided penetrating insight and blessed relief from irksome events that befall us all – at one time or another. "Viglets Two, Ode to Dumbness" is devoted to a more specific topic, but equally important, namely the happiness and joy of being dumb. For sure dumbness befalls us all - most of the time.

Webster defines, Ode, as a "lyric poem typically of elaborate or irregular metrical form and expressive of exalted or enthusiastic emotion." Webster also defines dumb as stupid. The author does however find this a bit over the top and much too harsh. So we will stick with the older and more compassionate form - simple - dumb. We all do need to cultivate tolerance and appreciate the dumbness in others.

Bingo – Viglet expressions remain irregular, always exuding enthusiasm and penetrating insight; this time they focus on the glory of being dumb, without rancor or placing blame, of which there is plenty to go around.

Dummies enthusiastically embrace dumb slogans that are basically quirky statements showing us paths leading to dumb outcomes. Remember? "Don't Shoot Till You See the Whites of Their Bloodshot Eyes" (anti gun controllers); "New Math – Forget Arithmetic" (frustrated parents and teachers); "Lose 53 pounds By Going to the Bathroom - Twice" (Rapid Transit and Home Depot); "No Child Left Behind" (Cruise Line folks and political educators); "No New Taxes" (Freedom buffs); " Time Heals All Roads" (Highway Pot Hole Departments); "Your Call, Our Church or Hell" (mega churches with big glass windows); "Support Compassionate Capital Punishment for All" (Overseas Drug Lords, Syringe Makers and Texas Governors); "Floss or Die" (ADA); "Neuter Your In-laws" (Society for Family Peace and Harmony); -- on and on. Actually some of these causes are pretty good, but only if you are dumb enough to fathom their deeper messages.

> *Dummies are never burdened*
> *By cause and effect relationships*
> *Their inspiration comes from Lady Luck*
> *Who often smiles on them.*

Many highly popular worthless books are written to help dummies, or so they proclaim. But really, how dumb is that? Dummies don't need or want help or they wouldn't be dummies. While these public supported educational efforts are psychologically maddening and philosophically whacky, the nub of this issue remains - what is the gut level nature of dumbness, can and should we do something about it?

Let us face it - we all know dumbness when we see it. Being and remaining dumb is not a matter of happenstance, no siree, dummies must work at it – and lo and behold – they do and remain successful.

So now it is high time we acknowledge, honor and treasure this purely human trait. Interestingly enough, other animals are not dumb like us, proving again that our species is unique. Humans may now confidently be viewed, from a purely scientific perspective, as being a dumb self destructive fluke, or knurled twig, wildly branching off from the same evolutionary tree trunk as everybody else. Truly, that is how dumbness came into being - a bad twist in the ole oak tree of life.

Every morning
Dumbness arises
Just like you, me and the sun
Another dumb dance begins
Tata – tata

Today we are constantly hammered
To ask our doctor about something
So - next time you have a check up
Ask the doctor about dumbness
See what he recommends.
Probably another HMO.

It is not often that evolutionary and creationist folks can agree, but this time it works. God did plant the "E" tree - but there were problems, He used the wrong kind of fertilizer (over nitrated), overwatered (He repeated this later with First Time Boater Noah) and failed to properly prune it (no prior gardening experience, His Schick was after all Big Kabooms).

What an occasion – here we finally recognize that being a bona fide dummy is prestigious and furthermore you get to demonstrate your talents, genetically obtained or learned, by creating and sharing dumb Viglets.

Seldom, probably never, has the genesis of dumbness been addressed in such a fair and balanced manner. Since Viglets are by far the most appropriate way to express and deal with key human issues it was decided to produce a definitive treatise on dumbness, offering the same clarity as was previously afforded "irkness".

Finally, from a practical, humanistic and realistic perspective let us admit.

*We have all failed
At so many things
So now it is time to
Do nothing and enjoy
Being a happy well adjusted dummy.*

Dumbness

Dedication	v
Introduction	vii
Joys of Being Dumb	1
The Case for Dumbness	9
Measuring Dumbness	19
Everyday Dumbness	28
Professional Dummies	37
Knowledge Management by Dummies	47
Leadership Roles for Dummies	54
Heritage and After Life of Dummies	61

Joys of Being Dumb

There is a lot of good to be said for and about dummies. They bring us endless joy as they effortlessly screw up just about everything that makes sense; at least we thought it did.

I was never very smart
And that was very lucky
Otherwise I would be in jail
Like all the smart ones.

However for us to continue enjoying dumbness we either enact more dumb laws or repeal the good ones we have. Of course, dummies should be able to drive on whatever side of the road they wish, for god's sake never signal, tweet everywhere, carry loaded AK-47s into kids ice cream parlors, blow smoke in the sky, ignore scientific evidence when it gets in the way of fun (thermometers are known liars), and finally, never, but never pay taxes, they are only for really poor who can easily afford it.

Dummies always make us happy and they are currently not in short supply. Luckily for us all, there is an endless stream of new ones coming right along – but, and this is a big but - only if these child bearing dummies stay away from electronic apps long enough to keep enjoying making whoopee. But we can probably rest assured our precious dummies are not that dumb. Nevertheless, hope does spring eternal.

However, on the horizon there appear ominous signs that maybe reproduction is becoming a secondary recreation for dummies, now including all of us who own computers. They (we) simply get, too engrossed in picking, pawing and stroking our apps.

Wouldn't you know it, Big Pharma (plural) has not lost sight of this predicament (they never do) and have now created a sweet, but not too sweet, smelling elixir to apply when your app suffers from "Easily Distracted" (ED) symptoms. You simply spray this yellowish goop on your app and they claim there are few side effect. This is not naughty talk. Without a cure for app ED – evolutionary results are not only dumb – they will be catastrophic for the growth of sorely needed future dummy generations.

It is indeed comforting to know that there are so many benevolent industries looking out for all us dummies. Their generosity and compassion is sometimes just too much.

Joy, Oh, Joy - we are constantly reminded of the British Bartender's quote:

> *"Viglets free dummies*
> *From today's tribulations*
> *Bringing joy and ecstasy.*
> *May I pour you a cool one sire*
> *While you enjoy a few?"*

*Many is the day
When I seem to be far away
So where was I?
Having fun being a dummy
With all my dumb buddies
At the pub - of course.*

*Being dumb is a great advantage
You seldom have to worry about the truth
Because nobody is dumb enough
To challenge you
So you are always the winner.*

*Creating a Dumb Viglet a day
Is essential for every dummy
It will keep personal troubles at bay
While bringing inner happiness
To you and all those about you.*

*Dumb Viglets are great
For healthy living
Create one and gone forever are
Crooked teeth, dementia, pimples and gout
If Viglets don't work
Call your doctor.*

Viggo P. Hansen

You know what?
If you are dumb
You better do something dumb now
Or somebody dumber than you
Will beat you to it.

Dumbness in politics is always fun.

Politicians have discovered that
Facts should never get in the way of fiction
They can use fiction to bolster facts
And the other way around as well
When it suits their fancy
To muddle the issue.

Creating personal Viglets on Dumbness will energize your inner life with happiness, by helping you poke fun at yourself for being just damn dumb – most of the time. Another way of putting it – be yourself, conjure up some Viglets and be happy with your dumb life. You got nothing to lose but your dignity and self respect – which were probably challenged to begin with.

With the passing of time, like bottles of ageless Two Bit Wines, your dumb Viglets will become priceless memories of your paltry life's struggle to remain happily dumb while fooling everyone else. This is equivalent to exploiting life while banging your head against a brick wall and feeling worse when you stop.

Please dear reader do not skip over these upcoming creative exercises – they are essential and guaranteed to preserve, maybe even enhance your dumbness with time. They will become an heirloom for your ancestors to cherish and be embarrassed by - how dumb you really were.

You have been given some solid information on the Joys of Dumbness and some encouraging Viglet prompts - now you can fearlessly created your own masterpieces.

Just keep in mind - dumb is beautiful and is meant to be appreciated, not denigrated or depreciated. You have earned this respect through a life time of being dumb. Furthermore, and herein lies true Viglet beauty – you are not hampered by grammar, spelling, dangling participles and other stultifying bookie stuff – just express your self – let it all hang out as they say – dummies do.

Space is now generously provided. Try to be neat so your Viglet will look beautifully dumb when you frame and hang it – again preferably in a rose wood frame.

Dumb Joy Viglet 1

Dumb Joy Viglet 2

Viggo P. Hansen

Dumb Joy Viglet 3

The Case for Dumbness

As you continue your exhilarating journey down the Viglet road of happy dumbness you must prepare yourself for all the wonderfulness this trip provides. First - a little ego builder Viglet.

Remember Newton, Isaac, that is
Who stood on the shoulders of giants
Well, we dummies too stand
But on the shoulders of dumber dummies
So be proud, stand tall, like Newt.

Always begin with an open and uncluttered mind, admitting to yourself that you are a true dummy who is lacking proper recognition. Few have ever fully appreciated how dumb you and, all of us, really are. That is about to change because now begins our moment of rapture.

I seem to fail at everything
But that is really not so bad
Think of all the poor souls
Who fail at nothing
They are the truly pathetic
At least you failed at something.

Since dumbness is so pervasive we must acknowledge it must have had an origin; probably upset gods, big bangs gone awry, or maybe bad smokes. Regardless, we must be thankful that dumb happened.

There are ten, possibly more, irrefutable reasons for dummies to rejoice. These are referred to as The Ten Dumbs, (TTD – today even dummies use acronyms)

1. Dumb One; It is easy to be dumb. For the majority, if not all humans (billions of us), dumbness comes naturally. As noted earlier, the evolutionary Homo sapiens's twig took a crooked twist eons ago making dumbness now viewed by some as a god given gift. Most religious leaders of our age seemingly don't understand this turn of events any better than the author.

2. Dumb Two: Dumb humans are entitled to a sense of arrogance. If in your dumbness you desire to have a superego that beats everything - go for it. People who are non-dummies are challenged because they cannot for the life of themselves see how happy really dumb people are – all the time.

Dumb people frequently walk around with a smile that says it all. So while the dummies are smiling (even smirking) the smarties are frowning and worried about what went wrong with their inherited genes, that now requiring them to chew Tummy and gas deflating pills.

Entitlement favors dumbness
Or is it the other way around?
Dumbness favors entitlement.
In either case everyone is a winner.

3. Dumb Three: Here is the best of all – Gods, real or imagined, must really love dummies because they keep making so many of us. It is said and widely observed that the dumb shall inherit the earth, which now includes, but not limited to, politicians, foreign chemical manufacturers, corrupt bankers, land mines, insurance companies and professional ball players. You can also argue that dumbness can be substituted for the (tut-tut) expression - original sin. This is one of those tricky, ticklish, theoretical, theological conundrums.

> "Religious Wars"
> Are surely Holy Wars
> Like Holy _ _ _ _Moley.

> The industrial-military complex
> Pales in comparison
> To the current religious-political cabal
> Is that dumb or what?

> Wars are great for economies
> Makes sense to spend money
> Killing each other
> Rather than conquering
> Diseases that can really kill.

4. Dumb Four: "Do-Gooder" organizations thrive on dummies. Indeed most would quickly go out of business if they couldn't count on dummies sending them money on a regular basis. So with the cooperation of good old IRS, who cannot legally tax these entrepreneurial endeavors, we dummies now

enjoy contributing to tax free institutions so we can pay more taxes. As a result we get glitzy edifices all over hell and gone that pay zippo taxes because their expenses with the not so dumb executives and their big time TV coverage is naturally deductible. How dumb is this, you ask?

We have all heard the old saying
To get rich you must not pay taxes
This has all the smarts
Of hard rocks under water
But it surely works
As long as we have enough dummies.

5. Dumb Five: Politicians rightfully fear dummies. This is not due to simple paranoia. The reason is simple; they truly are dumber than the dummies whose vote they seek. Thus they are constantly challenged to come up with really dumb leadership ideas.

To be politically dumber
Than most
You simply vote no
On everything
Thus belonging to the party of dumb.

This should not be viewed as suicide for dummies – often it becomes the ultimate badge of being politically correct.

6. Dumb Six: Big Box Stores love dummies. They generously provide delicious free food, usually no alcohol, to keep their customers smiling as they relentlessly, fearlessly and chatting loudly on cell phones circle the stacks, touching and feeling, all the while oohing and aahing exquisitely glued together shinny merchandise from afar.

As I gleefully wander the aisles
Of highly stacked goods I do not need
The dumb spirit in me arises
Yes – I must have one, if not two of each
What I really need is a bigger cart.

7. Dumb Seven: Sporting events freely provide in-depth mental exercise for dummies, both on the field and off. That is why many of them are lacking teeth and walk around like zombies with bandages in strange places, like over their eyes - but please note - they never cover precious tattoos in private places.

   When want-to-be sport heroes
   Lack blood and guts on the playing fields
   They get their jollies
   By dukeing it out in parking lots,
   Before and after the games –
   Doesn't much matter
   As long as their team's honor bleeds.

8. Dumb eight: Dummies tend to shun advice. This is natural because they already know it all. What a plus. The advantage here is that it cuts down on clutter, chatter and sanity. Their mantra is "Don't bother me with facts." Lots of thriving - "Sly as...a...." media stations now successfully subscribe to this concept.

9. Dumb Nine: Dumbness probably begins before childhood. However just being a kid enhances it while adolescence really energizes dumbness. And that is of course why dumbness tends to run in families – everybody's family. This we all joyfully experience when attending reunions ranging from

junior high graduates to those incredible family bashes.

Though dumbness may be inherited
It is not something to be ashamed of
You can easily enhance it
By not going to school
And simply watch TV.

10. Finally - Dumb Ten: – dummies must share dumbness – this is a bit heavy. Dumbness is not something that anyone should try to hide in a dark smelly closet, bug infested attics or dingy oily garages.

Being generously dumb is the gift
Dummies constantly must share –
With both sincerity and humility
Aren't they just too precious?

Pluses, dumb people are emancipated people, meaning they are never:

Jealous

They have nothing to be jealous about
Except their dumb activities

Arrogant

They have nothing to be arrogant about
Unfortunately this does not deter some

Worried

If their wine is red, white or blush
As long as it's got good old ethanol

Stressed

*About latest clothing fashions
Just so their rags cover private parts
But not too much.*

So there you have it – ten darn good reasons to celebrate dumbness by creating dumb Viglets. Whenever you feel dumb or depressed, like most of the time, just return to these ten key perspectives and rejoice. You are in the good company of billions of folks who understand and appreciate how truly wonderful being dumb really is. Keep in mind – it will not change.

Even the famous Second Law of Thermodynamics – entropy, scientifically alludes to dumbness. It eruditely states something about everything eventually running downhill and sure enough that is what dummies do best - except they are doing it now.

*Dummies see nothing amiss
By doing the same dumb thing over and over
They strongly support the notion
That practice makes perfect.*

Now it is your turn to create three Viglets dedicated to being dumb. You may use yourself, significant or insignificant others, just be sure they are dumb.

Space is provided so you can artistically display your dumb creations. If you are using an electronic device you can of course embellish your handiwork with, exotic fonts, garish colors, stolen clip art and even boop music. Just make each one real pretty to reflect your true dumbness.

Viggo P. Hansen

Dumb Joy Viglet 1

Dumb Joy Viglet 2

Viggo P. Hansen

Dumb Joy Viglet 3

Measuring Dumbness

Our wonderful modern world is full of metrics - we like to measure stuff, any stuff, just measure it, and make some "pie" charts, create power point comics and become a consultant. Basically consultants are either dummies with numbers or numbers with dummies.

While measuring dumbness is not easy
We all know it when we see it
It provides us with entertainment and opportunities
To create and use uplifting expressions, like
"How dumb is that?"

Walking when drunk is sort-a dumb
Riding a horse when drunk is dumber
Driving a car when drunk is dumbest
Phoning and twittering when driving is super dumb
You got to wonder what is coming next.

Viggo P. Hansen

> *What? Signal*
> *When driving?*
> *Hell no,*
> *Keep the dummy behind you*
> *In icy suspense as to*
> *Your next dumb move.*

Throughout history humans have valiantly struggled with establishing nationally accepted norms of dumbness. On the surface one would see this as a slam dunk assignment. You are either dumb or you are not. The problem with that simplistic definition is dumbness is not a simple binary issue. There are many levels of dumbness, from silly to profound.

> *At some miniscule level*
> *All measurement tends to be*
> *By guess or by golly*
> *And dumbness does help smooth*
> *All the fuzzy rough edges.*

Great and not so great measurement experts have tackled the dumbness metrics problem. Initially it was thought to be simple. Joe is dumb, Mary is not. But then there were the rest of us who enjoyed a wide variety of dumbness.

The metric system would seem to be ideal for this challenge, but then some felt, Oh no, we must continue to use ole King "What's his name" foot as the standard. There was some logic in this argument because ole King "What's his Name" always did have his foot in his mouth, like most dummies.

Initially it is agreed there is an undefined point dancing somewhere where dumbness begins. This was later proven incorrect, just like the Medieval geocentric theory. But early on it was accepted that dumbness increases - exponentially.

That means once you get started being dumb it becomes easier to get dumber faster. It also means you can use positive exponents to express dumbness. You can be dumb squared or dumb cubed. And if you are really dumb you are dumb to the nth degree. My oh my, isn't this fascinating?

Dummies correctly felt threatened that once a scale was determined for dumbness it would be easy to establish merit pay scales, allocate vacation time and kill all health benefits. Obviously some unions took a dim view of this unorthodox approach.

Take the inactions of America's Representatives, especially the House. Naturally they vote only so they can get reelected - this is dumbness squared, but then when they vote no on everything, even stuff they believe in, it becomes dumbness cubed. The dummy scaling system seems to works.

Politicians not only enjoy this numeric nonsense but will pay for it, using your tax deductible contributions. E.g. 32% of Gila monsters in the Texas panhandle don't wash their paws after going to the bath room, priceless information, and highly useful for the reelection of governors.

This politically exciting fetish over number misuse inevitably led to the nagging question; can we really measure how dumb ordinary people are as first hoped? It remained an enchanting idea and the only way to investigate this was to toss some money at it. Keep in mind these are funds that dummies weren't smart enough to "shelter" from the IRS.

So now we poor dummies are funding research to quantify how dumb we really are. You got to admit this has the ear marks of dumb. Not to worry, it gets dumber.

These pork belly funded researchers said they would begin by "reading" the literature to see what dumb stuff had already been done. Wouldn't you know it - those that could read found, not some, but lots of it - volumes to be exact.

What these researchers uncovered is that our intelligence score is denoted by something called Intelligence Quotient or Idiot Quotient (if you like), IQ for short in both cases. With any genetic luck and reasonable nourishment at all, you should be around 100, give or take 50 points, you know, standard and non-standard deviations. Now some really uppity IQ-ers cooked up something they call Mensa. If you are Mensa, you might have an IQ of 150 or a billion, but who cares?

However in the hallowed land of dummies this became both a threat and a challenge.

> *Dummies not to be out done by Mensa*
> *Used the time honored expression*
> *Dummies are no dummies*
> *And swiftly created Densa*
> *So for IQ's below 16*
> *Mensa finally lost its completive edge*
> *To Densa.*

When pseudo-psycho-scientists with this new perspective on intelligence, or lack thereof, tried to establish a metric for dumbness, known as the PDQ (Pretty Dumb Quotient), they encountered some really severe problems with the previous concept of measurement. This has ancillary issues for statisticians whose very lives are devoted to, and depend on, bar graphs; furthermore it is no coincident that's also where they do their best work.

Even dummies know measurement is comparing things to an accepted standard, be it English or metric. Recall examples from El-Hi days? A kilometer is part of how far it is around planet earth, which is impossible to determine, because the earth is just sort-a round and real bumpy in spots.

They also realized that ole King Whatsname's foot was a wobbly standard of length because it tended to swell when he drank too much, understandable knowing he was a Brit. Einstein's speed of light is a great metric, but nobody knows how to measure it, because time is also a questionable commodity to measure, because it moves so darn fast. Like, "When will that motor mouth politician shut up; I have got to go to the bathroom". It is times like these the term "how fast" has real meaning.

Metric or English are
Great ideas
Now we all walk around
With pockets full of various sized nuts.

Bottom line - there are no absolute standards for measuring anything and thus measurement is a "sort of by guess and by golly" endeavor. That is precisely why dummies are so good at it. They instinctively know, "Yeah, it's about from here to there."

IQ measurement is easy, rocks have zero and you go upward from there. However the Pretty Dumb Quotient (PDQ) is much more difficult, because there is literally no bottom to dumbness. So when these "New Math" well meaning PhD measurement types started to quantify and compare dumbness they ran into some horrific problems.

With no bottom there is of course no absolute drop dead value to dumbness. Shaken, but not defeated, they decided to start somewhere in the middle and then go up and down from there. This is like the old math number line where you have a zero somewhere and then you have positive and negative numbers around that. Folks in Askov Minnesota, where outhouses are the vogue, learn this plus and minus business at a very early age during the frosty winter mornings.

Boy oh boy, can't you just envision the hair rising discussions this PDQ proposal engendered with the ethically, morally and politically correct ninnies. An aside, ethically political, or politically ethical is definitely oxymoronic.

The end result in this search for a dumbness standard is that there may indeed be a dumbness scale, but researchers have not yet been able to establish one. In a huff they simply gave up and began studying America's national debt. Believe it or not they ran into the same problems, since they have a lot in common.

For now we are left with the following. Dumbness is clearly quantifiable and can best be expressed with adjectives instead of numbers. Most importantly, you can make up your very own vocabulary to express how dumb we each are compared to other dummies we know.

Now, dear reader, ponder ranking all your dumb activities – a great personal experience. Using this treasure trove create three great dumb Viglets and rank them.

Dumb Joy Viglet 1

Dumb Joy Viglet 2

Dumb Joy Viglet 3

Everyday Dumbness

Viglets are primordial, gut level, expressions of literally everything in our daily mundane lives, with or without computers and their ancillary apps. Unabashedly Viglets address all issues; dumbness to smartness, beauty to ugliness, power to weakness, happiness to sadness, truth to lies, politics to religion (often quite similar and difficult to distinguish between), females to males, tykes to adults, and so on. If you can think it - you can and should create a Viglet about it. They can be humorously uplifting while simultaneously addressing humankind's deepest issues like, what in hell will go wrong next?

However, for dumb people most of this is not a problem. They have learned to live with dumbness, because they found it to be quite satisfying – so why quit? Some might see dumbness as an adjunct to a blissful life where thinking has become an uninvited distraction.

Giving dumb people power
Is dumb – we agree
But giving smart people power
May just be even dumber.

*Arrogance and dumbness
Have a lot in common
But if you have to choose
Support a bona fide dummy
At least you'll get honesty.*

---

*Solving the problem of
No child left behind is easy
Dummy down schools
And they will all be behind
That is equality.*

---

*Speed bumps provide healthy eroticism for dummies
They love to hit them at 50 mph
Tossing everyone and their car high in the air
Landing in a crushing screaming heap
They have a smoke
And giggle till the wrecker arrives.*

---

*Sharing the road with dummy drivers
Can be an enlightening experience
But always smile at them, remember
They are either on a cell phone, twittering
Drunk or both.*

Viglets require people to actively think big (not a challenge for dummies) and be creative (much easier when you are dumb). Never blindly accept intolerable situations foisted by pundits, cranky bosses, zitzy teenagers, teachers, parents, CPA's, PTA's, preachers and politicians, who walk around clasping their lap tops like a rabbit's foot, hoping for good luck.

Viggo P. Hansen

Viglet authors, who daily struggle with their own proclivities and dumbness, find internal peace of mind that is rare in today's hurly burly world of itunes and ipads, not to mention cell phones. They are no longer victimized - they have found that illusive freedom with the nature of things, like Buddha.

> *Dummies have a high tolerance for pain*
> *Look around and you will see*
> *How painless dumb must be*
> *Like backing up on the freeway*
> *Because they missed their exit ramp*
> *While busily twittering.*

Though dumbness is certainly not rare, dummies are often unfairly taken advantage of by the unscrupulous among us, most notably banks, insurance companies and peddlers of grave sites.

But dummies have back up plans of their own, for example;

> *Dummies' strategy*
> *To even the playing field with*
> *Banks and insurance companies*
> *Is simple.*
> *Get a big home loan*
> *Buy lots of insurance*
> *Torch the bugger.*
> *What the hell - the Government*
> *Will bail them and*
> *Dummies get the insurance*
> *Everybody is a winner.*

Today, leading a successful everyday dumb life has never been easier. We have all kinds of nifty gadgets, especially electronic, that are ideal for pursuing an effortlessly free dumb life.

Look around any kitchen, cluttered with countless effort free devices, all needing to be plugged in somewhere and sucking up hapless electrons flowing innocently through a nightmarish labyrinth of wires needing to be "programmed", somewhat comparable to herding earth worms. Here is a typical case where dumb fun really begins.

Take the ubiquitous tin can opener, sharp looking device; it has an LED clock with endless adjustments designed by foreigners, who use a variety of different languages and cheap robots to help then put weird gizmos together for us dummies. This piece of work, i.e. can opener, has an incredible array of stuff that should make your simple task of opening a tin can much easier and life fulfilling.

So - you being dumb, buy a tin can opener at The Big Box, put it on Visa Cheap Card, take it home, plug it in, attach a tin can of Campbell's best rutabaga enhanced healthy tomato soup where you logically think the can should go. After all there was a tiny arrow – somewhere.

Boldly and confidently you slam your right hand fist down on that sleek looking stainless lever sticking out of the contraption's left side.

For dummies this is the point where real life experiences begin as the magic machine takes over. First of all, it has electronically sensed that you are really dumb, and to prove that it is right, you are initially dowsed with cold sticky rutabaga fortified tomato soup as the tin can recklessly whips around, spins into kitchen space, then loudly plumps on the table top all the while the lid keeps whirling round and round.

In natural reflex reaction you grab the lever, now slick with crushed tomatoes, and raise it, while loudly uttering at first a single non-Sunday school expression. Your large tattooed right arm response rapidly sends the entire contraption flying to the floor scaring the living bejeesus out of your precious newly spade twelve year old feral puddy-kat. The survival oriented cat madly claws at your exposed sun burned non-tattooed legs with yowls only a dying alpha male panther can make when confronted by a diseased rhino.

Unconsciously you begin creating an entirely new language, complete with vocabulary, syntax and wild gurgling sound effects. These are expressions ancient Sanskrit folks never envisioned and you yell them so loudly that the entire two hundred and twenty unit condo complex now share your unhappiness with a modern day tin can opener.

Electronic alarms are going off everywhere, kids crying and dogs yelping. Only drunken husbands (significant others) for blocks around, busily drinking beer and engrossed watching Wednesday morning rerun football, clearly comprehend your pithy statements - some even courteously respond in kind, by telling you to shut the hell up, their team is about to score, albeit two weeks ago.

Instantly, using satellite media, your tin can opener saga has been spammed to the entire world. Russian, Chinese and Danes are on U-tubes busily reporting the event to CNN busting news. Fox said it was too hot to handle – right?

The saga is a hoot; dummies everywhere are rolling over in hysterics, many wanting to know where you got that marvelous tin can opener machine. Big Box is busily ordering more from exotic faraway places with Visa sending out new mailings of free no interest forever cards. When markets again open they will be bullish on tin can openers.

Let us analyze this common everyday situation and create an appropriate calming Viglet. You were truly dumb enough to buy a tin can opener that had been designed by and for dummies. The dumb engineers who had created this "device" relied on you simply buying it, couldn't figure it out and in frustration put it away for another day – no returns or law suits.

They relied completely on your dumbness to make money for overseas investors. A Viglet.

> *I often demonstrate my dumbness!*
> *Today I showed it by buying a tin can opener*
> *Made by dummies like me*
> *From over the sea*
> *A simple can of tomato soup to be opened*
> *Has now authenticated my dumbness*
> *That led to divorce and eviction by the landlord*
> *But for sure I am now a happier dummy.*

How about those new nuclear time keeper devices that never need setting?

> *A nuclear clock*
> *Does not go tick tock*
> *You learn to tell its time*
> *By how beautifully*
> *You glow in the dark.*

As dummies bravely face daily challenges, some but not all of their own making, they have a special lackadaisical aptitude to "go with the flow" – they instinctively know this is not the end of the road for them; bumpy though it may be for the rest of us. This is most admirable and will probably insure their survival, just like the planet's ever present pigeons – who just keep bobbing their heads as if they know what they are doing and by golly expect to live forever, regardless.

So, like the pigeons, it is now your turn to remember three dramatically dumb experiences and create a Viglet for each.

Viggo P. Hansen

Dumb Joy Viglet 1

VIGLETS

Dumb Joy Viglet 2

Dumb Joy Viglet 3

Professional Dummies

As to exactly what constitutes a profession is hard to determine, but for sure everyone, dummy or not, is now a professional.

> Professions may be viewed
> As clusters of dummies
> Who cleverly create
> Acronyms for fear that the masses
> Will find out their unholy secrets.

A safe bet is that on special occasions bunches of like minded dummies will get together over a beer on a dark stormy night and concoct a name unknown to others.

First item of business for professionals is to design resumes and business cards that tell it all. This is a challenge.

> Resumes of dummies
> Read like bad mystery novels
> Plenty of incredible heroics
> But no corpse is ever found
> Instead pages of accumulated tidbits
> Beginning with early toilet training.

Professional classification schemes probably began when cool (more likely cold) French cave dwellers dressed in sheep hides made scratchy squiggly lines on mildew covered walls. This activity may very well have been the origin of Viglets.

Luckily for these creative dummies this early "art" caught on, expanded and soon developed what is today known as the "Professional Arts".

In this twenty-first century anybody with a piece of chalk, a bucket of paint, or who can bang two rocks together without inflicting excessive pain on themselves is a bona fide "professional artist"'

> *Art is in the eye of the beholder*
> *It is fairly agreed*
> *But the question remains*
> *Whose dumb head?*

Since this is a family book on Viglets we will omit elucidating on the world's oldest profession. Suffice it to say that this profession has always been shrouded in a mystique regarding its internal system(s) of communications, using common terms like John, Mary, Spot, etc. to convey secret information. It seems to serve all levels of dummies quite well, especially politicians and statesmen. No wonder it is the oldest.

Moving along we find that terrified mountain and desert people, seeking to appease their upset gods and goddesses, started chopping up healthy living beings, some human, to get at the heart of the matter. If that didn't work they would simply heave them over high cliffs, while singing jolly good songs. These creative behaviors were later to evolve into the medical and theological professions.

While most gods and their goddess
Are concerned folks
Simply seeking, devotion, honor and respect
Medical gurus are seeking to pay green fees
And Priests continue singing feel good songs
All have a lot in common
They want to help us dummies
Thank you all!

Clinical evidence indicates that
Dumbness does not seem to swell the brain
It has just the opposite effect
It shrinks it
Which is abundantly evident to everyone
But the patient.

Once the swelling subsides
Said my doctor
You may notice side effects
That we don't understand
But that is to be expected.
After all we are only doctors.

There are dummy doctors
Who often get mixed up
About how and were to incise
Their solution is simple
Cut from both front and back
Or up and down
Hoping to meet in the middle.

※

Psychologist's love to say - "I see"
Problem is too many of them are
Blind to the real problem namely
Most of us are blind dummies.

Some places on earth bipeds with strong backs piled big rocks on top of each other to look like enormous triangles. Others made long elevated winding rocky roads where they could stand and shoot arrows at strolling passersbys. All became professionals at their tasks, today we call them engineers - many are still piling rocks. In Askov, MN they dig the rocks out of the ground to make piles, how quaint is that?

Throughout history eating has always been a concern of dummies. There is corroborated evidence that on occasion clusters of dummies would decide to beat up on the cluster of dummies living next door for eating smelly foods rich in garlic. These became known as Italians, because of Italian cuisine.

Dummies who now engage in these eating endeavors are professional chefs and nutritionists. They will always have a tasty nutritious yellow rutabaga sauce or colorful pill for any occasion.

Dining is fine, but
Eating pills, like lots of them
Beats cooking vegetables and
Fixing dead animals
Pills let your guts shrink
Minimizing flatulence
Allowing you to keep poking at your computer.

The bookkeeping profession is ideally suited for dummies. Here is a true Viglet submitted by a cheating taxpayer who was being audited by IRS for the sixth time in two years for simply posting his gains as losses. Though this is a common practice among major corporations, it is certainly frowned on for small business and individual clients. This deadbeat decided to express his frustrations in a clever Viglet.

I had this dummy CPA
Whenever I got an IRS audit
He generously gifts my agent a box
Of foot long Havana cigars
And is then confused as to
Why we lose – easy answer
He should have given marijuana.

The famous professional Sir George Dunghead, III, MBA, DOA, CPA, Senior Dumb Fellow and chief economist for the GODP (Grand Ole Dummy Party) is worthy of study. Among this trusted friends (both of them) he was best known as " Sir".

"Sir" could jimmy books and locks
He wallowed in paranoia and narcissism
His body mass to height was three digits
His only two pals were in jail
But alas Sir George III
Was sadly only a borderline dummy
When it comes to modern banking schemes
And so he too ended in jail.

Viggo P. Hansen

Beginning at the dawn of history, and still practiced in our modern world, the gentler sex decided long ago to douse themselves with perfumes, made from stuff you don't want to know. They would pour this strange smelling liquid over their sweaty stinking gorgeous bodies, rather than taking time for an occasionally good soapy shower. These professional perfumers have always ranked high with dummies and the reason is obvious.

While showering is a bore
Smelling like one may be worse
Better douse your body
With odd juices from hither and thither
Smelling good leaving a trail
For others to follow.

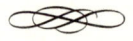

Beauty is in the beholder
Vanity is egos on steroids
Dummies enhance both
By seeing their perfumer.

Professional farmers (agribusiness men) are sometimes paid generously not to farm, thus helping to keep the cost of food high so poor people can enjoy the virtues of starving. This looks dumb on the surface, but it sure helps keep elected "farm" officials in office so they can keep on subsidizing their electorate.

Said Farmer Bill
We must devise a way
To not pay taxes
We will use tax deductible devices
Like simply saying no to crops
We can then be subsidized, tax free
Just like our big boys
In Washington DC.

Often when belonging to a "profession" members have to: wear outlandish clothing (head gear that often resembles animal body parts or elementary school dunce caps); sometimes required to grumble in strange tongues (probably because of being drunk); and eat funny things all the while humming captivating mantras, like hoo ya, hoo ya, go team go.

You undoubtedly have had some exhilarating personal experiences with "professionals". These priceless moments ranging from pure ecstasy to utter frustrations can now become immortalized by your Viglets. You know the drill – you have three opportunities to express in - Viglets - professional dummies and dumbness. This is the easiest lesson in the book.

Dumb Joy Viglet 1

_____

_____

_____

_____

_____

Dumb Joy Viglet 2

Dumb Joy Viglet 3

Knowledge Management by Dummies

Time to address one of the most perplexing posers of all times, namely, how do dummies manage knowledge? There are of course inane quips like; they don't, why should they, they haven't got any, who cares, etc. But these hurtful comments are neither nice nor always true, they only confuse the issue.

What is true is that many institutions, some even of higher learning, whatever that infers, are now in all seriousness offering courses, degrees, certificates and colorful placards along with a free box of dumb nuts on the topic of knowledge management. You have got to admit this is pretty darn clever.

> *Creating and managing knowledge*
> *Is never a problem for dummies*
> *They know that it doesn't matter*
> *Whether the planet gets warmer or colder.*
> *They will comfortably remain calmly dumb*
> *And stay in politics.*

Whenever dummies, or whomever, seek to manage knowledge they surely are drawing a fine line between being a liar and a truth teller. More than likely once you start "managing" knowledge you have unknowingly slipped into the liar's den, but what the hay, you already have papers hanging on your

Viggo P. Hansen

walls testifying to being a manager, meaning you do what you want to by being selective, i.e. managing to suit your whims. Truth can be pesky at times.

However it is in these murky waters that dummies excel.

> Dummies say
> Those who know it all
> Are indeed unlucky
> because they'll never
> Enjoy the thrill
> Of learning more.

> It is yapped about
> That Edison tried a
> Hundred light bulbs
> Before one worked
> How dumb was that?
> I only wish I was that dumb.

Ever since universities and colleges arose many have become centers of learning - so they tell us. If someday you are bored with life in general check out university catalogs and start reading course titles: "Theories of Fiction" (stay away from truth), "Thinking" (dah), "The Planning Idea" (very clever), etc.

> Dummies with super egos
> And there are lots of them and us
> Can be truly magical
> As well as entertaining
> If not taken too seriously.

If dummies don't know something
And they often don't
They will cook up something really dumb
Like knowledge management
And then sadly discover
They have little knowledge to manage.

Military ventures (or miss-ventures) provide lots of examples of dumb knowledge management. Remember that guy Hannibal taking elephants for a Sunday ride in the Alps? What a show to watch!

"Get the damn elephants in a line"
It is up the hill we must go
Barked The Mighty Hannibal.
Why? I am not sure
But it somehow fits our long range
Military strategy plan.

Designing weapons of mass destruction
How truly dumb is that
Unless you are really suicidal or
Have a badly inflated ego
Needing a crutch.

Building fighter planes at great expense
To fight non existing enemy fighter planes
Is surely dumb – No?
Alas, not for dummies.

Viggo P. Hansen

We must constantly be reminded that everyone, dumb or dumber, really mean well – it is just that we are all so dumb we can't understand it. Be compassionate – it is for yourself.

This assignment is easy – create three **Viglets** on how you experience dummies (and they are all around you) managing their knowledge and generously sharing it with others.

Dumb Joy Viglet 1

Dumb Joy Viglet 2

Dumb Joy Viglet 3

Leadership Roles for Dummies

Inevitably the role of leadership comes into every discussion on the future of dumbness and international diplomacy, they have a lot in common. Without dumb leadership, dumbness would suffer. While nature abhors a vacuum, dumbness cannot survive without dumb leadership.

Dumb people
Make great leaders
That is why we pay them so much
But what about us who
Chose them?
We must be even dumber, yes?
And we surely get paid less.

The dumber you are
The more people want to follow you
While the smarter you are
The more people see you as a threat
So rejoice in being dumb and
Enjoy your devoted audience
You may be their dumb leader
And don't know it.

It is essential that leaders arise and provide the necessary visions for the future survival of dummies. A positive outlook is helpful. Consider the following: A well known dummy, simply known as Ditsy Dee Dingbat; coined the following Viglets.

If you don't learn from your today's screw ups
There is a good chance you'll redo them tomorrow
With even more spectacular dumb results
How great is that?

Genius is my business, said Ditsy
Doesn't pay well
But what the hell
I am genius.

At one time this was actually pretty sound thinking. Ditsy Dee Dingbat, had been a twentieth century popular dumbness guru performing staff devilment (spelling is correct) workshops around the world.

Ditsy was especially respected for her politically successful failures, but then in despair she drifted into studying ancient philosophies of the Antarctic and junk bond futures. She nearly won the Nobel Award for her incredible and incessant overuse of Power Points.

Ditsy was a knock-out proud dummy
Could excite the dullest of the dull
With glowing tales of riches
By simply using her drop dead
Dumb Power Point (DPP) presentations.

Viggo P. Hansen

But alas the poor dumb Ditsy ended up a broken nitwit doing a life sentence in an igloo with no wifi and scads of other brokers and insurance agents.

It has always been a problem for leaders who, as they become successfully dumber quickly lose their sense of humility and soar into grandiose bravado. This is particularly evident in weepy wallowing politicians, whose only job is being reelected as an ongoing dumb politician. Be compassionate – they often cry when they loose.

The following Viglets resulted from meetings recently held throughout the Great States of Iowa and California.

Oh, please dear dummies
Elect me before it is too late
I solemnly promise you that
I will remain dumber than you
Till my next election.

President Ike warned us
About the military industrial complex
Some said then he was dumb
Today we better worry about
The political-religious cabal
Which by the way is even dumber!

Leadership may be priceless, but dumb leaders, aside from being a disaster, do provide us with lots of gallows humor. At this crucial time in global history, when we are up to our yoo-hoos in dumb leaders, we much too often fail to appreciate what a treasured resource these twits will be for future historians. So - how dumb are we? Unfortunately his stuff can get real serious in a hurry, even for Viglet authors.

VIGLETS

Civic leadership
Is the highest calling for any dummy
So when in office
These dudes will define their tasks
As dumb as they wish
And we stupidly believe and follow them
Hardly funny.

The opportunity for you to expound on the dumbness of our glorious leaders is now. Simple mull on the dumb leaders you know, but be sure you first have a cool libation. Remember, just thinking about our leaders often leads to either uncontrollable laughter or self mutilation.

This time we encourage you to first write the names of three really dumb and laughable leaders. Toss back a couple of drinks and have at it.

Dumb Leader 1. _____ DL 2_____ DL 3_____

Tough decisions, eh?

Dumb Joy Viglet 1

Dumb Joy Viglet 2

Dumb Joy Viglet 3

Heritage and After Life of Dummies

There is only speculative and inferential evidence that dumbness may not cease when dummies enter their next life. These circumstances are of course dependent upon how dummies behaved, i.e. lived out their dumb life while they were here.

Many theological possibilities are imaginable, from being reincarnated as a mindless skinny slippery newt to a ravishing well hung jersey cow. Others will naturally seek and have different options depending on past experiences and religious proclivities. Unfortunately you still can't google this.

It is certainly possible for dummies
To be either naughty or nice
Though some may be confused about this
We can all agree
They always do what comes naturally.

Having been certified dumb all my life
I am at least consoled
By the fact that I had a life
Among so many fine dummy friends.

Viggo P. Hansen

⸻

Getting old dumb
Is payment for being dumb young
But you know what
It was worth the price
It never changed my life style.

⸻

Dumbness learned over time
Augers well for a gloriously dumb future
That we have all justly earned by
By supporting dummies and being one of them.

⸻

When dummies dream
They dream big
The action is all theirs
With them at the center
Doing all the dumb things
That makes us laugh, cry and scream.

⸻

When all is said and done
Dumbness may have won
That of course simply means
We are all winners.
Tata

Let us be reminded by the following Viglets how fun it is to be dumb and to anticipate a glorious future that may be even dumber.

*We all did lots of dumb things
When our minds were young and agile
But when we got older and our minds got fragile
We now do even dumber things
Thus we must be careful
Never to get old – that is really dumb.*

---

*Reward for dumbness
Is eternal happiness
Where we will all live in
Blissfulness dumbness
Driving on the wrong side
Of streets paved in gold
Gleefully laughing
That we had beaten hell.*

The future of dumbness is like the big bang, it just grows and grows – bigger and bigger. So here is another opportunity to create three beautiful **Viglets** expressing your wishes for a bright hereafter for all dummies – and don't forget to include yourself.

Viggo P. Hansen

Dumb Joy Viglet 1

Dumb Joy Viglet 2

Dumb Joy Viglet 3

Onward and Upward Vigleteers

The concept of pervasive dumbness is perhaps only an illusion that we sense and/or practice as we struggle with our own daily irksome activities. Some of these oddball "dumb" behaviors may - hopefully - be mere oversights; human foibles as we say. However when they result from selfishness, greed and avarice they are no longer simply cute. They become gross and demean the human potential for being tolerant and "nice" to each other.

We are today lots of folks on a small, indeed very small, ball whipping around in space that we do not understand. But we can understand and practice being considerate of each other – being less "dumb", eh?

Our brief journey into dumbness has hopefully been for the most part; enlightening, spiritually fulfilling and even joyful. We have all become better human dummies, meaning fewer middle finger salutes, less vulgarity, more happiness, but - we still have zippo tolerance for those inconsiderate idiots (not dummies) who never signal and constantly chatter away on cell phones in inappropriate places.

Future Viglet voyages will explore expanded vistas and unknowns. Until then be a Happy Vigleteer, gleefully surfing on an ocean of dumbness.

ABOUT THE AUTHOR: Viggo P. Hansen

The author has enjoyed an abundant life rich in personal experiences with dumbness. He began his exhilarating journey by being born into a poor Danish immigrant family homesteading in the plains of Eastern Montana, stolen from Native Americans. The Great (not so) Depression provided an opportunity to leave dust storms in the plains and go to H.C. Andersen School, milk cows and hoe rutabagas in Askov, Minnesota. He served without distinction screwing nuclear bombs together for the US Air Force, fortunately with no mishaps. Attended Grand View College, University of Minnesota, became a professor at Cal State Univ. Northridge, CA. Wrote math books and voted in all public elections on a regular basis.

His life as a dummy and working with them has given him keen insights into the true nature of dumbness and how manifest it is globally – now seemingly growing at an exponential rate. In his current unemployed status he wishes to share his unsettling knowledge by helping everyone associated with dummies create personal dumb . His overly doting lovely wife Dixie, Point Loma garden guru, thinks he is nuts, but that is their personal and sensitive issue.

His thesis is simply: "Since dumbness abounds and seems to be very healthy, we must learn to understand it better, share personal dumb experiences while enjoying our collective dumbness and forgo all statistics created by politicians".

CPSIA information can be obtained at www.ICGtesting.com
Printed in the USA
BVOW07s1806130714

358972BV00003B/250/P

9 781467 062459